Nurse

Adult Coloring Book

Safe, Silly, Snarky Swear Word Mandalas
For Nurses, Nurse Practitioners & Nursing Students!

Amusing Sayings for Work, Home, Nurses, Doctors & Patients

Geez

La Allergies!

Sugar Honey

Iced Tea!

Heavens to

Hemorrhoids!

12 Hour Shifts

are for the Birds!

NO FROWNS

FOR CODE BROWN!

Blooming

Barnacles!

Dang

Vital Checks!

Made in the USA
Columbia, SC
07 May 2020